Vocation

Yasmin Djoudi

Published by

Nine Pens

2021

www.ninepens.co.uk

ISBN: 978-1-8384321-9-5

009

Contents

Delayed British Airways Flight London to Algiers

My seatmate says *Whitney,* mouth in a pinch.

Blood sacrifice.
Illuminati.
Fact.

Let me out! a child screams —
or perhaps *Let me in!*
It's hard to tell which.

Night flight by force.
The length of the segmented ceiling becomes
the pale belly of mutiny crouching above.

She tries to display, in the cold cabin light,
certain proof on her phone. Whitney flees from the screen;
in the glare it stays tinted as black SUVs in the night.
Seatmate pivots to improvised themes.

Engaged to be married, fiancé, *here, see* —
she waggles her hand, shows a rock like the chip
of a bottle smashed onto the hull of a ship.

Her surprising profession —
she's *in aviation,*

and springs into data on global emissions.

Seventeen percent maritime — listen —
just twelve from planes! Remember that next time

THEY do their campaigns, and shame you for flying . . .

Her ears pick up whispers on airwaves:
the stirrings of *THEM.*

It's the hostess who gives her a sneer,
or the British crew, tight-faced, serving contempt
as they do *every Africa flight;*
or the girls of Algiers.

In this country, the women are vicious.

Back prime to be stabbed;
morals not what they seem.
Private beaches and thongs—

you don't know what I've seen.

And she's sizing me up now.

Staying for long?

Sleek nail taps *new contact.*

I'll drive, come along . . .

       Where this went, could have gone, I won't ever know.
          Her number's a ghost ship in my broken phone.

Sakana

They swiped me in Tokyo three-thirty this morning,
straight from the bay and into the bath. The tiles
are white as my succulent flesh. Slice me: veins of fat
tell you I'm good. Only top quality, fresher than dawn.
Find me this morning. See how I'm swollen:
it's only because of a change in the pressure. Throw me
in water and see how I wriggle, seasoned and warm,
like tears.

Then

brushstrokes
of
crickets

        scratch
        night into
        indigo

                a silk
                morning
                dress

Hothouse Flower

Blooming hibiscus probe the dark greens.
Discs of lush rubber beg for a squeeze.
The atmosphere bulges with humidity.
Forgotten, a plant sinks right down to the crocks
that sit sharp in the base of its pot.
Crimson, it rises. It dares to grow strong.
Its buds close. It feels its own poisonous roots.
Long-legged attendants twist down the trees
to fight for the honour of pruning its leaves
with their very own pincers, clicking in lauds.
It grows. The plant hits the roof of the hothouse.
A group passes by. It hears a hush fall.
They're looking. Admiring. Just as perceived,
Fate. All the lonely nights gazing at stars.
Astonish in passing, strike awe in the commons;
you may approach, Fate, what took you so long . . .

Behind glass, the group hardens time frames.
Setting their schedules and mouths, the plant
is given a sentence. Outside.
Ice webs on the panes. The silver threads tie.
One weak winter morning they come for the plant,
a sheet and a shovel as palanquin.
The chill is sufficient to kill a daydream.
They grunt. The plant is too big for its pot.
Won't wilt. It shivers, it perks up — it bursts —
they reel from a great crescendo of musk.
The plant, sensing eyes, slipped out of its skin.
Its grateful mouth flashes its teeth.

Vagrants

spotted
autumn
suckling
fear
berlin
gangways
whining
steer
half heard
reports
of world eating

rifling
shadows
shoulders
scree
snowchain
ruminant
scourge

sanguine
the heart
made of woods
at the core
they remember
forget them
they come
when
called

Weekend Break

I move through drunk Americans like the delivery guy at a party looking for somewhere to put this pizza down

A sex shop stares back at me while I'm browsing for bras. Evening shoppers, sedate pac-men, carefully avoid its sphere of influence...sex shops are always the elephant in the mall

In a private room I take a selfie then weep — don't wake the dormitory — time for midnight goulash!!! Meaty, rich, and brown, I make it later far away and scald my teeth with vinegar

The city is captured by a sinister golden mask; its drumming arms compress our chests; devils and bears, camp followers, now run amok, beset by history and novelty dildos. Heels echoing round an austere corner, I stumble upon a man and a woman wearing matching trench coats

I am frowned away by an antiques shop in my faded green boots. The dress shop is oddly desperate for me to stay. The tall blonde slopes towards me at the same angle as her eyebrows

In the frozen morning I buy out-of-season fruit and suspect I've been short-changed

Passage

White contrail threads eye of new skyline —
reconstruction slipped over the past like skewed nylons.

Bird strike on grey country road, skidded thin,
tracks up the valley like hair on the skin.

Thunder's tin mug scrapes the bars of his jail.
Put out your hand. No shocks here — just hail.

Central

i rush into central a nude down the staircase
no time to stay housebound and roasting a
chicken we get in the uber we fly on red
carpet i'm rolling a pumpkin from soho to
baker street endless walking from soho to
baker street back again hoping at zero to
sixty and buying new jeans in carnaby street
i master my emails while wearing them
often i feel i'm transforming i'm starting to
mutate i download the app and delete it
again stuck in a flickering circle of coyness
i'm giving up noble and plumping for vain
nightly routine where i lie down in traffic
inflamed faces running across the terrain
of the jesus is optional walk it off quick
clean the bathroom another eruption of
strange on the cctv solid gold on the rails
a suspicious new lattice of fractal mistakes
and everything falls apart right into place

Stewardess

Each day I wake up and pour out the coffee
I think of the journey   I put on my shoes
and avoid my reflection   I creep
like the moss down the pavement   I smell
dirt in my hair   I top off with hairspray
solidity is luxury   I'm a lighthouse
in the subway   I am bundled in grease
an uneasy foundation   I render my face
look at my uniform   tight as an orifice
I swing your censure   I progress polyester
a hushed benediction   I step out on plastic
dirtied with the footsteps of the world
no doors can buffet me.

Reptile Song

some beat their fists
on the wardrobe

crocodiles lie on the bed   patient leather

saltwater crocodiles
swim in the sea

swimming for miles   they're essentially dinosaurs

crocodiles swam
to the tropical islands

swapped catching waves
for coconut water

                              slightly threw up on the
                              fourth long haul flight

                              nicotine gum in the
                              watering hole

                              touch on the chin to swing
                              open the jaw

having such terrible trouble
with teeth

vision of running
in uneasy sleep

through luxury rooms
full of thousands of clocks
thousands of clocks
wall to wall
ticking clocks

and cold blooded woke
from a crocodile dream

salt is a well known home
antiseptic

do not remember
the taste of the sea

Missed Flight

Opal eyes, said Patti.

Blue plait, said Patti.
She was describing the wife of Rembrandt.
Patti spoke with the tone and control
of the best televangelist.

Two beds in the room,
a large dog named Bo,
a two-ticket email I printed alone —

but first,

Tom and his girlfriend met me at the station.
In greeting, I instantly stepped on his toe.
Too tall for their own good, the Dutch.

For my imposition as surrogate child,
doing my best as a last minute thank you,
I bought a bouquet from a canalside florist;

also, old postcards with someone in mind
in an optimist's tour of a series of markets.

(All of the postcards, historic or kitsch,
remain in a box in my parents' attic.)

Patti invited two giddy young girls
onstage at the end of the show.
I ate some sweet morsels called poffertjes
at an altar to football disguised as a bar.
Taxied back home, nosed in greeting by Bo.

I occasionally hold up this topic in private,
letting the truth catch the light.
How opaline, feminine friendships.

Estate

Decor stripped everywhere,
slumped in relief,
as if to say phew, off the clock girls,
time to unhook and hang free.

Indecent as the city in peacetime:
spread-eagled on stone, tinsel boa tossed off;
only the breeze buttoned up.

Spring, newly sober, a sensible freshmint
keeping at bay her sticky late pastimes
of cider and whisky.

Thank the solicitor, walk out the door,
share a hasty goodbye in the grey April light,

a kiss at the ruin over your shoulder—

drinking spots   *fanning scripts*
kitchen smog   *weed and chips*
manic outburst   *skin on bricks*
bare mattress   *a stranger's tits*
the dotted lines   *a heart must know*
the stage floor   *scent of stale playdough—*

and you still haven't climbed that wretched volcano—

Taxi!

He's trying to take me home I can't remember where I live
He's bouncing hip hop off the windows as we shoot
by three young men They're wearing camouflage in blue
and standing next to sweeps of concrete white austere
they're plain in view as stubborn as my lack of tongue
The driver turns back in frustration but we mutually gape
We're sliding jellyfish on freeways only option is the window
sweating purple at the monuments in shared tourist despair
Dead silence flatly punctuated by Novoy no um Novotny...

Honey

the holy month
the danger is named
golden it drips through the cracks
you open your mouth to small kisses of breeze
after sunset dried fruit
sickly sweet strangely dusty
the stream rustles softly
outside the hotel rooms
the empty restaurant
the barman is shy
he is polishing glasses
he slowly describes all the outdoor attractions
a white plate in front of you oily with salmon
you could ask him for more
you could swipe from the river
whole families of salmon
and crunch their bright scales into silver fillings call it
just doing your job
but outside it smells clean
it is night there is no one
the same linen dress
now creased flat to your shape
alone on the bridge
you sniff down at the water
it licks the flat stones scrabbling for its own moisture
you know in the dark waiting over the hill
in the dark like raw honey unpasteurised honey
deep in forest unseen there are squadrons of men
in their guard posts who watch for the packs of wild beasts
they are loyal equipped with all things that are hard
they are there to take aim at the bears

Extremities

Noon, the hour of Englishmen.
The underpass leads to the beach.
I need a mad dog.

Sewers.
Waste.
Nodding blue cranes
portside drink from the stench.

Dip. Up for air. Dip down again.
Come up for air, where it smells just the same.

Cargo ships cross the strait.
They're leaving thick trails
of the stench in their wake.

I bait waves in a red swimsuit.

Roommate

I receive shocking news that I have a body. The body's a stranger I met in a café, asking if it could please use the seat opposite. Now it's my roommate. We share a small studio.

I never wash up. I never do dishes. The body comes home every night and cooks offal. It stinks up the studio, smashes the plates.

We walk in the space. We stay in the moment. I realise I'm having an—*'ow you say*—breakdown. I escape down the street past the lines of blue shutters. The body, it follows me to the patisserie. Shrug with the baker. I chow down. Puff pastry. I choke authenticity—body, it follows. I flee to the studio— body outflanks me. Body is panting, the panting is eager.

I walk through the door and the body is waiting. It sits in the chair in the empty white space.

How I hate the body, its flair for dramatics.

I'm asking the body to give me some space.

I shout at the body. It doesn't respond—and then sprints at me, clutches at me like a toddler. I'm telling the body I don't want a body. It stays there and listens, dumb meat.

Long lunches. I order blue steak with the body. I say to it, isn't this you on a plate. We're sitting outside, puffing under space heaters.

I say to the body, inhale.

One night I wake up. Sudden light in the hallway. The body is standing there, black in the doorway. Its gaze pierces me. I can't read its expression.

It tells me to try falling upwards.

Giving Up

When God closes a door,
He also remembers
to close all the windows.

Light stunned the box room
through plane trees in late summer.

I threw myself against locked doors
like a bird in a conservatory.

At least a small wound makes you interesting,
like those pigeons with one foot turned into chewing gum.

Lockdown Birthday

Another darkling year, a blackbird in the bush,
a tighter ponytail, an outfit gone to waste.
I'm thinking of the time we walked around this park,
committing to the rain. To memory, I suppose.

As the light is fading, around the outdoor gym
pure white socks and trainers take flight like yuppie birds.
I keep my ears pricked up. Juicy conversations.
. . . and I'll have a sauna . . . don't indulge *in women . . .*

The world is on the fritz. Nowhere to go but out.
I let my hair down, wet, hoping it's going to dry.
The plug pulls on the sky. Far headlights spark the gates.
They blink into the dark, then slowly turn away.

When I was seventeen, I sat below that tree
and muttered sour vows to make my great escape.
And I've been there, done that. I still found something wrong.
Nostalgia's like the sun. Don't look at it too long.

Sauna man, now cycling: *I'll tell them of the word!*
The word of Jesus Christ! What does it mean, return?
Here, trying my hardest, with hands off handlebars,
I'm grateful I'm alive. I'm trying really hard.